Octopus

Melvin and Gilda Berger

SCHOLASTIC INC.
New York Toronto London Auckland Sydney
Mexico City New Delhi Hong Kong Buenos Aires

Photographs: Cover: Jeff Rotman/Photo Researchers, New York; p. 1: Max Gibbs/Oxford Scientific Films, Oxfordshire, UK; p. 3: Jane Burton/Bruce Coleman, Inc., New York; p. 4: Newman & Flowers/Photo Researchers; p. 5: Mary Beth Angelo/Photo Researchers; p. 6: Jeff Rotman/Photo Researchers; p. 7: David Hall/Photo Researchers; p. 8: Mick McMurray/Seapics.com, Kailua-Kona, HI; p. 9: Zig Leszczynski/Animals Animals, Chatham, NY; p. 10: Mark Deeble & Victoria Stone/Oxford Scientific Films; p. 11: Sophie de Wilde/Photo Researchers; p. 12: David Fleetham/Oxford Scientific Films; p. 13: Eiichi Kurasawa/Photo Researchers; p. 14: Max Gibbs/Oxford Scientific Films; p. 15: Rudie Kuiter/ Oxford Scientific Films; p. 16: Rudie Kuiter/ Oxford Scientific Films.

Book design by Annette Cyr

ISBN 0-439-47391-8

12 11 10 9 8 7 6 5 4

3 4 5 6 7 8/0
08

Printed in the U.S.A.
First printing, March 2003

Meet the octopus.

Fun Fact

The octopus has no bones in its body. It is able to squeeze into small spaces.

The octopus has a soft body.

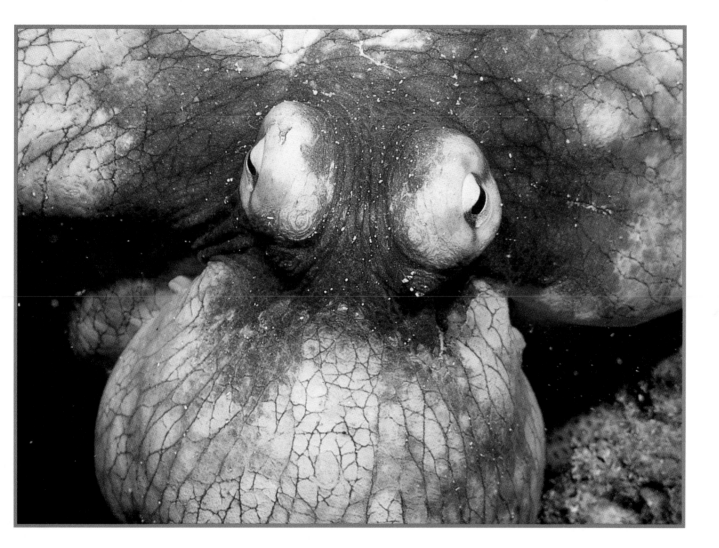

The octopus has two large eyes.

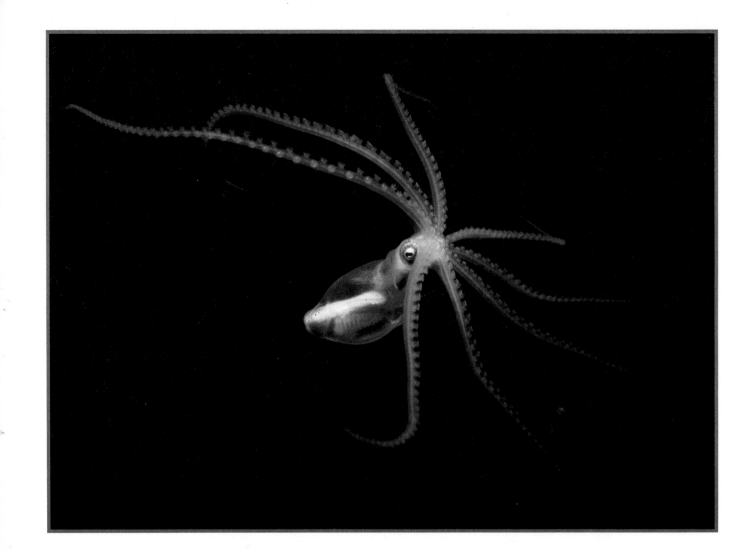

The octopus has eight arms.

Fun Fact

If an octopus loses an arm, a new one grows in its place.

The octopus uses its arms to move about.

The arms catch food.

Fun Fact
The octopus eats crabs, clams, and mussels.

The arms carry food
to the mouth.

The octopus can be big.

Fun Fact

The biggest octopus is more than twenty feet across. The smallest octopus is less than one inch across.

The octopus can be small.

Fun Fact

To swim, the octopus shoots out a jet of water. This pushes it forward.

The octopus swims.

The octopus hides.

Fun Fact

A female octopus lays more than 100,000 eggs at a time!

The female octopus lays eggs.

The mother octopus
cares for her eggs.

See the baby octopuses!